~~~ The Harmonic Convergence ~~~

~~~ The Harmonic Convergence ~~~

MICHAEL ALLEN COOPER
WHAT I SAW

The Harmonic Convergence
Copyright © 2016 by Michael Allen Cooper. All rights reserved.

No part of this publication may be reproduced, stored in a retrieval system or transmitted in any way by any means, electronic, mechanical, photocopy, recording or otherwise without the prior permission of the author except as provided by USA copyright law.

Scripture quotations, unless otherwise indicated, are taken from the *Holy Bible, King James Version*, Cambridge, 1769. Used by permission. All rights reserved.

Scripture quotations marked (KJV) are taken from the *Holy Bible, King James Version*, Cambridge, 1769. Used by permission. All rights reserved.

This book is designed to provide accurate and authoritative information with regard to the subject matter covered. This information is given with the understanding that neither the author nor Imperium Publishing, Inc. is engaged in rendering legal, professional advice. Since the details of your situation are fact dependent, you should additionally seek the services of a competent professional.

The opinions expressed by the author are not necessarily those of Imperium Publishing, Inc.

Published by Imperium Publishing, Inc.
1097 N. 400th Rd | Baldwin City, Kansas 66006 USA
www.imperiumpublishing.com

Cover design by Samson Lim
Interior Design by Manolito Bastasa

Published in the United States of America

ISBN: 978-1-64318-025-0
1. Religion / General
2. Biography & Autobiography / Religious

Contents

Introduction 7
The Honeymoon's Over 15
A Bolt of Lightning 19
Sheol 21
The Witness Pleads 25
The Harmonic Convergence 29
The Black Box 33
Motive 37
Expedient 39
Am I My Brother's Keeper? 43
O, That Smell 47
Discernment 49
Lit Up 53
Stilts 57
Plan A 59
Dialogue 61
Vision 63

Introduction

I looked into a slice of time one night during a dream, and I was shown two angelic beings that were watching God the Father. He was quite a ways away, but distance was not an issue. It was as if He were right beside them. In the far distance, the universe twinkled and was like a moving and living entity. Swirling, and yet still. Black, yet full of small lights that shined and reached out in all directions infinitely. The Father was standing on nothing at all, and yet it was a surface of invisible rigidity. He was bent over a rounded boulder. The two beings were also seemingly standing on nothing, but it was not an issue.

The two were very beautiful and yet plain looking with human features. They radiated light, love, and concern. They wore long flowing robes that covered their feet. Their hair was clean, shoulder length, and combed. They were paying attention to every move the Father made and yet talked to each other face-to-face. One said to the other, "What's the Father doing over there?" The answer came at the same time, "I know, he's been hovering over that area for a while."

They didn't have to walk to move, they just moved at will. They both came toward the Father to get a closer look. It was fluid movement, and without time loss, even though it was a great distance. Distance was not an issue, and lack of atmosphere wasn't an issue. The universe seemed totally small, though it was what we call millions of light years across. The small boulder that the Father was looking at seemed like it was four foot across. It was hanging in mid-air, and it was black and by no means perfectly round. It was like a rough rocky black sphere, with no features that could distinguish it as anything special. "Void, and without form" (Gen. 1:2, KJV).

I can't tell you the hundreds of thoughts that were going through my mind, but I can tell you a few that seemed to rise to the top of the list, like what is this place? Who are the two beings? Why can I see this? Is this the creation? Like I said, too many to enumerate and process, and yet the answers were right there with the questions. Simultaneously.

The Father was shaping and molding the sphere with His hands and hovered over it with an intense purpose in mind. He was preparing it for the future work He would do. He looked up at the two angelic beings as they approached. They are the Word and the Spirit. They are one with Him in all that He does and have been with Him always. His eyes were full of love and compassion. His depth was more than I had ever seen. His vastness was more than can be written. Many have touched upon it, and yet it is more than infinite. We will never get to the entire end of it. He is infinitely wise and loving. He is willing to share this wonderful thing called life and love. He knows that there will be a price to pay for sharing it, and that it will be misunderstood, misused, and abused. His decision that it is worth it came long before this day of creating. His determination won't be swayed nor questioned. He had already set out and completed His mission to expand this universe infinitely to see if there was any other gods before Him. He found none. He knew all the things that needed to be imbedded into the scene to make it successful. He was the first and the ultimate physicist. He didn't miss even one detail or facet that needed to be considered. All things were ready now, and He spoke with authority as He looked at the sphere.

He said, "Let there be light," and there was light. The sun appeared a short ways away from the sphere, even though we call it ninety-three million miles. For Him, it was just an arm's length. He also created the moon. He divided the light from the darkness by spinning the sphere with His will. He called the light day and the darkness night. The evening and the morning were the first day.

The Father said, "Let there be an expansion in the midst of the waters, and let it divide the waters from the waters." The expansion was made into two parts—the water on the earth and the water in the atmosphere. The Father called the upper part heaven. The evening and the morning were the second day.

The Father said, "Let the waters under the heaven be gathered together unto one place, and let the dry land appear." It happened just the way He spoke it. He called the dry land earth, and the gathering of the water He called seas. He saw that is was good.

The Father said, "Let the earth bring forth sprouting, herb yielding seed, and the fruit tree, yielding fruit after its kind, whose seed is in itself." It happened just the way He spoke it. And He saw that it was good. The evening and the morning were the third day.

The Father said, "Let there be lights in the expansion of the heaven to divide the day from the night. And let them be for signs, and seasons, and for days and years. Let them be for lights in the expansion of the heaven to give light upon the earth." It happened just the way He spoke it. He also had made two great lights; the greater light to rule the day, and the lesser to rule the night. He also made many more stars at that time to help light the night. He saw that it was good, and the evening and the morning were the fourth day. Now all that was in a small forty or fifty-foot circle for the Father, but we here on earth say it's millions of light years across. It was also in moments of heavenly time;

mere seconds. "One day is with the Lord as a thousand years, and a thousand years as one day" (2 Pet. 3:8).

The Father said, "Let the waters bring forth abundantly the moving creature that has life and fowl that may fly above the earth in the open expanse of heaven." He created great whales, and every living creature that moves, which the waters brought forth abundantly, after their kind, and every winged fowl after his kind, and He saw that it was good. He blessed them, and said, "Be fruitful, and multiply, and fill the waters in the seas, and let fowl multiply in the earth." All this happened just the way He spoke it.

The Father said, "Let the earth bring forth the living creatures after his kind, cattle, and crawling things, and the beast of the earth after his kind." It happened just the way He intended it to be. The evening and the morning were the fifth day. Then the Father turned to the Word and the Spirit and said, "Let us make man in our image, in our likeness, and let them have dominion over the fish of the sea, and fowl of the air, and over the cattle, over all the earth, and every crawling thing that crawls upon the earth."

The Father formed man with His hands out of the dust of the ground, and breathed into his nostrils the breath of life, and man became a living soul.

The Father planted a garden eastward in Eden, and He put the man in it to cultivate it and keep it.

He also put the "tree of life" and the "tree of knowledge of good and evil" in the garden.

A river went out of Eden to water the garden, for it had not rained upon the earth yet.

The Father said to the man, "Of every tree of the garden you may freely eat; but not of the tree of the knowledge of good and evil, you shall not eat of it: for in the day that you eat of it you shall surely die."

The Father turned to the Word and the Spirit again and said, "It is not good that the man should be alone; I will make him a helpmate."

The Father caused a deep sleep to fall upon Adam and he slept, and He took one of his ribs out and closed up the flesh. With the rib He had taken out, He made a woman and brought her to the man. Adam said, "This is bone of my bone, and flesh of my flesh, she shall be called woman, because she was taken out of man." That is why a man shall leave his father and his mother and cleave to his wife, and they shall be one flesh.

The Father said to them, "Be fruitful, and multiply, and replenish the earth, and subdue it, and have dominion over the fish of the sea, and over the fowl of the air, and over every living thing that moves upon the earth. Behold, I have given you every herb bearing seed, which is upon the face of all the earth, and every tree, in which is the fruit of a tree yielding seed; to you it shall be for food. And to every beast of the earth, and to every fowl of the air, and to every thing that crawls on the earth, wherein there is life, I have given every green herb for food." The Father saw everything that He had made, and, behold, it was good. The evening and the morning was the sixth day.

The angels in the heavenly realm were just behind me and watched with great anticipation and wonder as this all unfolded before their very eyes. They could not understand it all and certainly didn't know what to expect next. There were oohs and aahs and shouts of praise throughout the large crowds of angelic beings. The chief musician undoubtedly cued the rest of the praise team and songs of praise sounded throughout the area. Hallelujah to the Great God of the heavens. Who is like unto you, oh God of us all, Creator of the earth and sky, Lord of all humanity. There is no one like unto you. We worship and adore you. We bow ourselves before you. Angels choirs singing, hallelujahs ringing. We love you, Lord, and we lift our voice to worship you, oh our souls rejoice.

It seemed to be never ending songs of praise and worship, and for this cause, they were all created. It was the ultimate fulfillment for each one. Only during the praise and worship were their hearts full of joy and love. A real sensation of elation. The most for His Majesty was the gift to be given and received. No greater gift can they give or receive than to lay down their life for the one who had created them to have such enjoyment as this. There is no greater height or better feeling than to pour themselves out as a drink offering and be drunk by the eternal Father of light and love.

Then flowing back to repeat it time after time in a new and better way than before. Each time growing and gaining more of the eternal power and knowledge. Cycling in and out of the ultimate joy of the universe. Glory without end.

Meanwhile, back on earth, Adam and his wife Eve were naked and unashamed to be in the presence of the Father and each other. Adam undoubtedly showed his new mate all the garden and explained all that he had heard from the Father. "We can eat any fruit we want except for the fruit from the tree of the knowledge of good and evil," he told her. He fully understood that they were not to eat it, and he in fact told her "not to even touch it, or she would die."

The Honeymoon's Over

The honeymoon must have been going very good for a time. The Father would come by each day in the cool of the evening to visit and fellowship. After a while, when the new had worn off a bit, apparently, they would go places without the other one. One day, when Eve was off by herself admiring the tree of the knowledge of good and evil, she had a visitor. It must not have startled her when this visitor spoke to her. It wasn't Adam, and it wasn't the Father. It was a serpent—a serpent! Subtle. Slow. Slithering along in the garden, and it spoke. It spoke? Yes, it spoke her language. It asked her a question. "Hath God said, you shall not eat of every tree of the garden?" She replied, "We may eat of the fruit of the trees of the garden: but of the fruit of the tree which is in the midst of the garden, the Father has said, 'You shall not eat of it, neither shall you touch it, lest you die.'" The serpent said to the woman, "You shall not surely die. For God doth know that in the day you eat of it, then your eyes shall be opened, and you shall be as gods, knowing good and evil." The woman then noticed that the tree was good for food and pleasant to the eyes, and a tree to be desired to make one wise. She took of the fruit and did eat and gave some to Adam and he did eat of it also. Then their eyes were opened (to good and evil), and they realized they were naked.

Note: They could see okay before and had 20/20 vision. But this new seeing was more of an awareness. They sewed fig leaves together and made aprons to cover themselves. Later they heard the voice of the Father walking in the garden in the cool of the evening. They hid themselves in the trees. The voice of the Father is like a waterfall resounding, and a chorus of birds singing, with a mighty rushing wind to usher it in and out. The beauty of His still small voice will woo and comfort like no other. There are no words in our language to accurately describe it.

I love the way the Father asks questions that He already knows the answer to. It demonstrates the gentlemanly quality of free choice that He has given us. We have every opportunity to tell the truth or to evade the truth.

The Father called out to Adam and said, "Where are you?"

Adam said, "I heard your voice in the garden and I was afraid, because I was naked; and I hid myself."

The Father said, "Who told you that you were naked? Have you eaten of the tree that I commanded you not to eat?"

Adam said, "The woman that you gave me. She gave to me of the tree and I did eat."

The Father said to the woman, "What is this that you have done?"

She said, "The serpent beguiled me, and I did eat."

Now I just want to pause for a moment and say that there are many chapters and books written about all the reasons that the woman and man ate. They may or may not carry weight with you and I, but for this small glimpse, it doesn't matter. I want to explore why the serpent was there in the first place, could speak to them, and why he did what he did. At this point in the Scriptures, when Eve answered the Lord God Almighty, He wasn't surprised or shaken. He gave them freewill and free choice on purpose. He knew this would happen and what He would do about it from before the creation. He had already purposed in His heart that it would be worth it and that He Himself would pay the price to redeem the humans.

Immediately, when Eve answered, the Father turned to and said to the serpent, "Because you have done this, you are cursed above all cattle, and above every beast of the field. Upon your belly you shall crawl, and dust shall you eat all the days of your life. I will put hostility and opposition between you and the woman, and between your seed and her seed, it shall bruise your head, and you shall bruise their heel.

He spoke directly to the serpent who was apparently in the close vicinity watching what would happen to the humans that he had just lied to and lured in to get them to eat of the tree that was forbidden. How is it that the serpent had understanding and language? How is it that the serpent was so convincing and yet bold with his lie?

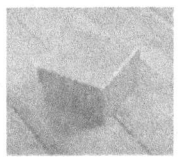

A Bolt of Lightning

"And He (the Lord Jesus) said unto them, 'I beheld Satan as lightning fall from heaven'" (Luke 10:18).

Now the first several times I read this passage, and for many years, I just presumed that He meant that He had seen it right about then. But lately, I have been wondering if He was just making a statement that had happened at some point in history. Not that day. It could have been before or after the creation of this earth. Jenzten Franklin shared a message on television that it happened on the day that Lucifer quit praising and worshipping. That has some heavy merit to it. He folded his arms and refused to worship. Bam! Out of there like a bolt of lightning. He had been the one that was zealously praising, and then said in his heart; I will ascend into heaven, I will exalt my throne above the stars of God (Isa. 14:13). It was at some point before Lucifer took on the form of the serpent and tempted Eve, with the idea that the Father had held back some knowledge that she would want. That serpent was not truthful about the situation. The Bible calls Lucifer the father of all lies. He told the first lie and continues to lie. One third of the heavenly host believed him and chose to follow him. That too was not a surprise to the Father of mercy. He had given them freewill and free choice as well. The decision by Lucifer to exalt himself above the throne of the Father was a fatal one to say the least. It will cost him his eternal joy. It will cost him his eternal ability to worship and praise the Father of all love and wisdom. Now keep in mind, we were all created to do that. Worship and praise. We can't truly be happy unless we do just that. I know there are many ways to praise and worship, and I hope you have found a way to give honor where honor is due. When we bow down and give homage to the Father, we truly find ourselves and the inner joy that we seek. Peace, love, and fulfillment. The things we really desire. We will never be satisfied until we worship the Father, the Word, and the Holy Spirit. It is our true calling. It will fulfill us in every way.

Sheol

Isaiah 14:15 makes it clear where that bolt of lightning winds up—the inner core of the earth for now. Lucifer will be cast into the lake of fire, prepared for him and his followers. "Hell has enlarged herself, and opened her mouth without measure" (Isa. 5:14). We were not made for hell (absence of God and His Holy Spirit), but we choose and our choice has consequences.

"I made the nations to shake at the sound of his fall, when I cast him down to hell with them that descend into the pit" (Ezek. 31:16). "But, whosoever shall say, you fool, shall be in danger of hell fire" (Matt. 5:22). See also verses 29 and 30. "But I will forewarn you whom you shall fear: Fear God, which after He has killed has power to cast into hell" (Luke 12:5). The rich man went to hell. "And in hell he lifted up his eyes, being in torments" (Luke 16:23). This illustration goes on to tell that if a person won't believe Moses and the prophets, then they won't believe even if one rises from the dead; they won't believe Mike Cooper either, or will you? I would give my life if you would just believe and receive Him as your savior. Jesus (the Word) already gave His life.

"For if God spared not the angels that sinned, but cast them down to hell, and delivered them into chains of darkness, to be reserved unto judgment; and spared not the old world, but saved Noah the eighth person, a preacher of righteousness, bringing in the flood upon the world of the ungodly" (2 Pet. 2:4–5).

My note: Many people worked for Noah and heard him witness about the flood that was coming. They didn't believe it. Until the water swept them away. "And whosoever was not found written in the book of life was cast into the lake of fire" (Rev. 20:15).

Our name was written in the Book of Life before the world began, and it could be blotted out due to our wrong choice. Choose wisely.

One moment in hell would explain many things to us and convince us that we don't want to go there.

A million years in heaven will only whet our appetite to want more of the mercy and love that only the Father of Abraham, Isaac, and Jacob can give us. Seek Him while He may be found. He's just a whisper away from you.

Jesus is the Word of God; the Father incarnated into human form.

John said it well. First John 1–5. Look it up and read it.

That which was from the beginning, which we have heard, which we have seen with our eyes, which we have looked upon, and our hands have handled, of the Word of Life;

For the life was manifested, and we have seen it, and bear witness, and show to you that eternal life, which was with the Father, and was manifested to us;

That which we have seen and heard we declare to you, that you also may have fellowship with us: and truly our fellowship is with the Father and with His son Jesus Christ.

And these things we write to you that your joy may be full.

This is the message which we have heard from Him and we declare to you, God is light, and in Him is no darkness at all.

The Witness Pleads

For many years, I have and still feel that sense of urgency to tell as many as possible about the good news of Jesus the living Christ. His coming is even right at the door. It has been that way for close to two thousand years. Peter spoke about it back then. He said, "Brethren, we are in the last days." So I think that now we are even closer to that last day, when the trumpet will sound and the dead in Christ shall rise, and then we who are alive and remain shall be caught up with them in the air and so shall we always be with the Lord. When I think that He took the time to come to earth and give His life as a ransom for us all, I can barely contain myself. We can boldly enter His presence and have fellowship with the Father of life. Well, I just can't contain this information from going out, and I am overwhelmed with the joy He gives.

Whether you live to be the ripe old age of ninety plus, or die tomorrow as a young person, will not matter if you belong to the Lord. If you are walking with Him, you can't get lost. He knows the way since He is the way. You just follow Him, and the destination is irrelevant. The final walk will put you into the heavenly realm with all your loved ones, ancestors who made it, and kindred spirits who love you and that you can enjoy eternally. You will be able to trust any and all that are there and never be hurt or cause hurt again. We were created to do a certain work, and unless we do that, we aren't satisfied. The deep longing in our heart cries out to worship the ultimate God of the universe. The world has cheated many out of the fulfillment we can have in that. We have not taught our children to seek that yearning we all have. Even the church fails to really get it. They instead have allowed religion to take hold. God reaching out to man really works. He has shown us what is that good and perfect work. Man reaching out to God has failed over and over. One good example was the ancient tower of Babel. All the deacons of the multitude got together and decided to build a tower up to heaven. It was a mighty undertaking that would let them commune with the God of the universe. It all seemed logical to them. But it was foolishness in the sight of the one true God. People wound up with different languages and went their separate ways and left the tower unfinished. If a person just walks off alone for a few minutes, repents, and humbles themselves, and asks God to come and talk with them and walk with them, He will do it. He says He will do it, and He doesn't lie like a man. It may take more than once. He may want to know if you really mean it, or if you are just testing Him. He knows the difference. Don't try to test God, He has already shown His character throughout the ages. The key to connection is true humility and a repentant heart. If this is not present in you and you want it and know you need it, then do like David and many others did and ask God for it. During your time, He will develop it in you if you continue steadfast. Be patient and seek His ways. Be quiet and listen to Him. Turn off the TV, the radio, and the noise around you. There will be plenty of time to hear other stuff later if you choose Him. Over the years, I have learned to enjoy the quiet more than any sounds other than His voice and directions. When He speaks, it penetrates your soul and calms the heart and mind. He speaks truth and positive direction. He has comfort and love in His voice. It reminds me of a waterfall that is close by; so full that it dominates all the sound around you. It seems to come from all directions and can't be overridden unless you yell. Why would you want to yell though? It just ruins the moment.

The Harmonic Convergence

One night during a dream, I saw many of the men that I was mentoring in the drug and alcohol program. I was encouraging them to seek the Lord and instructing them in His ways. I too was being encouraged by the Lord Himself, and He said to me, "Look up now and see, it's a harmonic convergence." When I looked up into the north part of the night sky, I saw a large spiral staircase that went up miles and miles into the heavens. It was huge and made of light. It had many colors of light in it and was radiant. It was many miles around, and sounds of beautiful music were coming out of it. People were gathering and going upward on it. I told the group of men to come on now. It is time to go. Most of them just kept lying around and watched TV. Some were milling around in the basement. Some of them came and looked and turned back, and some kept coming with me. We were headed to the stairway by then. Once we got on the spiral stairway, we didn't have to walk anymore. It was like an escalator moving us up. As we got up higher, we could see many others whom we knew. The excitement was so thick we became almost giddy. Spells of laughter and praise were definitely the rule and not the exception. My heart breaks for those who doubt and decide to not come to the call of the Lord. The call is going out in this late hour. "Come to me all who labor and are heavy laden, and I will give you rest," says Jesus our Lord.

Maybe you have something in your mind that says "due to this particular thing, I will not seek the Lord." It could be anything from the fact that innocent children are being killed and harmed, or people are starving. Whatever it is, you have this reason that you hold onto for not connecting with or wanting to understand and love God. You have a grudge against Him. You say, "If God is so loving, how come He allows this to happen to innocent people?" The Scriptures are clear on this: God did not intend for the inequality, nor does He cause it. When the humans in the garden chose to disobey His command about not eating of the tree of the knowledge of good and evil, they inadvertently allowed evil into their (and our) world. We can justify almost anything in our mind, but the fact remains that God did not desire for the evil to be part of the eternal realm. He did, however, know the choice would be made by man. Even some of the angels who knew the entire scope of things would also choose the evil side too. So it's clear that He allowed it. This one fact, if applied to the entire plan, will allow you to understand that even though God did not desire it, He did allow it to be a part of it. This way, it will never happen again throughout the millennia of millions and billions of years. We will be able to have complete trust. We will all know the final results of certain choices. I often say, "I know what not to do." I don't always know what to do, but it seems like I usually know what not to do, because I already tried that and it didn't work out. Since we know the final outcome for certain choices, we avoid making those choices, and it will be even easier in that world that we'll soon see. It's God's city; not mine or yours. We will inherit all that He has for us; adopted in as real sons and daughters, with full benefits and all His glory, wisdom, and honor. Words cannot express, the eye has not seen, the ear has not heard, nor has it entered into the mind of humans what good things He has in store for us that love His appearing. We long to see what the sons of God will appear to be on that day when we are made whole.

The Black Box

Here's a small scenario to envision. See a small black box on the table with one side open, but it's still black inside. You can't see down in there, and you don't know what's in there. You can only imagine. You watch someone walk up to it and they stick their hand in, and it cuts it off clean to the wrist. Now they are yelling and hurting. They are holding their wrist with the other hand, and they run away bleeding and in great pain. A few minutes later, another person comes up and inspects the box, and they too put their hand in and it cuts it off. Well, you are sure now that if anyone puts their hand in the box, it will be cut off. Another person comes up, and this time, it's a young child. He puts his hand up to explore the black box, but you intervene and say, "Don't put your hand in there, it will cut it off." He looks at you like you have a third eye in your forehead. He doesn't believe you, and you can see it in his actions and his looks. What he decides at that moment will either leave him with or without two hands. Some would put the hand in no matter what you said. Some might wait and put it in when you are not looking a little later. You might or might not stay right there to guard the box. Some might listen to you and heed the warning and believe you. Now you know for sure the box will cut your hand off, and you might even be one of them who now only has one hand due to the fact that you had put your hand in. You might have no hands at all due to the fact that you are stubborn and wanted to see if this thing is consistent or not. You can test this box millions of times, but it doesn't get full nor does it quit lopping off hands. It just keeps on cutting them off. A decision has to be made by all those who come in to contact with this black box. The process in the mind will not determine the outcome of whether or not the box cuts off the hand. It cuts off any and all hands that go into it regardless if they believe it or not. Now you know it, and some others know it, and eventually all know it. Time will tell the truth of the black box and its rules. Rule number one: it cuts off hands. Rule number two: you can't change rule number one. So you tell others, and you write about it. You put up signs, and you even stand guard a lot. You write cool songs about it, and they are loud and clever. But it's inevitable, some are going to stick a hand or two in. You even notice that some bring others up to it and force the hand of innocent bystanders into the box. How unfair is that? You are livid. You would like to rectify that, and you start proclaiming to all who will listen that you will not tolerate anyone forcing someone else's hand into the box. Alas, it has little or no effect. The deed is still going on. You want help so you solicit others to take a stand with you. Some do and some don't. You have a whole group now, and the number is growing incrementally. You all feel very strongly that this practice must stop. You even invent different ways to proclaim the truth. The reality is that the black box cuts off hands. But there are still groups that are starting to outnumber your group, and they drag others to the box and force their hand into the box. Their hand is cut off. You knew what was going to happen, but due to many other circumstances, like time, distance, ability, you were not able to prevent it. We all watch. Some are okay with the practice and some aren't. Some just accept it as part of the daily routine. There are those that cheer it on and get a thrill out of it. Condone it. Purport it and want more of it. The table seems to have four sides, and they come from every direction. You are on one side or the other, you can't be neutral on this issue. You have feelings about it no matter what you say out loud. Deep inside, you make judgments. There is a line in the sand, and you choose where you stand on this and every issue known to man and God.

You have rows upon rows of categories that you base all things on. One line is built upon another. If a line somewhere is shown to be false or misappropriated, then it affects all the other lines up and down from that. There is no fact under the sun that you cannot decide on. There is no neutral zone in this universe. Choose wisely.

Are you content with allowing God (who knows all) to make the decision for you? Do you trust Him? Do you think that He will do the right thing? Would He be able to make sure a book says what He wants it to say? Could He be the author of the Bible? Can He instruct men to write what He wants them to write? Is His power unlimited? Did He create this universe? The earth? The people? Anything? Everything? There is no neutral zone in this universe and everyone must choose the side they are on.

Motive

Motive is a word that underlies all that we are and believe to be true. It may or may not be appropriate, but that's another part of the story. We all have motivations, reasons, and beliefs that underlie all that we do and say. There came a time when I had to start evaluating my motives. Were they okay? Or were they inappropriate? I asked myself scathing questions for many years to seek my basic purposes for doing or saying what I did. I studied the Word of God to get insight and instruction. I asked the God of the universe to please intervene in my life if I was off course or wrong. I asked Him to intervene even if I was right. You can be right or be happy, choose wisely. I asked Him to guide me and help me in the search for truth and wisdom. Even though I was not faithful at all times, He was. He never forsook me or left me to be cast out into outer darkness. Our choices carry the weight of our eternal destiny and our immediate direction. If I was on the wrong course, I wanted to know and correct it as soon as possible. There are prices to pay for veering off course. We miss certain opportunities and either avoid or collide with certain things in life. All due to our choices. Minute by minute, we make a choice. Hour by hour, we abide in the choice we made. Hours turn into days and weeks and months. Scales can form over the eyes. We can become thick-skinned about certain choices and keep ahold of them even when shown they are wrong. Be careful what you choose. Consider your ways. Even though you're wrong, you can turn from it and be renewed in mind and spirit. The consequences are not inevitable until later when they are. I would rather allow that open channel to the truth than be stuck in my stubbornness. Whether I am right or wrong, I will not be stubborn and set against new insights that I may be shown. The many facets of truth go endlessly into the future, and we learn to build upon that truth. It can be a sure foundation that lasts forever.

Expedient

Shortly after the day of my conversion to being a believer in Jesus the Christ, I had old friends come by the house to see if what they had heard was true. At first, they would act like they were just visiting for no particular reason, or some would offer some pot or other drugs to see if I wanted them; but soon, it would become clear that they were curious about the rumors circulating around town. Some folks told me about them and would repeat them to me. "Have you heard about Mike Cooper? He's a Jesus freak now." Many people were shocked to hear this due to the fact that I had been somewhat well known for sports and then for being a drug dealer. It was news that a small town loves to talk about, and many of my friends either wanted to test me on it, or just hear about it. One particular friend knocked on my door at about bedtime and of course wanted to visit like it was the old days of staying up half the night drinking. He came in, and we visited for a bit. At some point, I felt like I had Jesus perched on my shoulder, and He said,

"Tell him about me." I recognized that voice immediately as the voice of the Holy Spirit, and so I started looking for a way to introduce the Lord into our conversation. It didn't take very long for the cue to come; I knew this was the moment. I started telling him in my own words what had happened to me a few weeks before that. It was not exaggerated nor hyped up. It was just the plain truth of the event that night. Jesus had spoke to me and showed me a little of the separation that hell has to offer. He then continued to show me what some of the comforts of His heavenly realm offers. He was direct in His approach and didn't try to make it seem like it was anything more than it was. This is what I also do since then. State the facts and then allow the other person to choose. So that night was no different in any sense of the word. I simply told the guy what had happened to me, and then he told me that this was awesome news. He was so relieved to hear that the story of Jesus was true. He had been living in doubt and just wanted to know if there was some reality anywhere. For the two hours that we visited that night, he heard the facts of my conversion, and we prayed together. A couple days later, I heard that he was in a car accident and was killed. Needless to say, I had questions and asked the Lord, "Why?"

My pastor, Orvil Holden, took me under his wing for years. One of the first things I remember him doing is setting up small meetings for people to hear my story. At one such meeting, a couple of my old classmates attended. I was surprised at the interest they had. The one young man had been active in church for many years while growing up and had fallen away from his faith in Jesus. He was living in sin and laughed at the things sinners laugh at, like serving the living Christ. He asked me many questions that day, and I remember the message I was impressed to give. The Holy Spirit had been very succinct to me about the message. It was based on a Scripture found in the New Testament. "You do not know what will happen tomorrow. For what is your life? It is even a vapor, that appears for a little time, and then vanishes away" (James 4:14). A week later, Orvil organized a citywide revival meeting at the small lake in our hometown. He rented a flatbed trailer and borrowed some generators and brought the sound system out, and they played some good old-time gospel songs, and then he had me share my new testimony. Half the town of Gillette was there it seemed, and I felt the Holy Spirit come over me to anoint my words and to embolden me. I told them about the vision of hell and heaven that I had seen and the darkness of being alone forever. As I looked into the crowd, I was aware of the same young man whom I had spoken to about the brevity of life. He told me later that he had made a new decision in his life. I also ran into his mom the next week, and she was thrilled about the return of her son to the faith. A week later, he was killed in a car crash.

A few months later, I was married. And shortly after that, I had contracted a drywall job out of town. I was asking around to see if I could recruit some help to hang and tape a house. One of the men who I asked was my younger half brother, Bobby, and he agreed to help me. He also had a couple of drinking buddies who would be willing to go. We would be camping in the unfinished house and roughing it since we couldn't afford a room. For a few months, I had been telling Bobby about Jesus and His wonderful attributes. He would listen, but had no interest in actually going to church or reading the Bible. We four went to the out-of-town job and started hanging Sheetrock. Days went by, and each night, we would roll out our bedrolls to sleep on the floor. We worked from early morning till dark thirty. The third night, we had just went to bed about dark, and we talked for a few minutes, and then it went quiet for some much needed sleep. I felt an evil spirit come into the room, and it was an eerie, heavy, and sickening feeling. The whole room was full of the fog of it. I immediately prayed in my inner self and said, "Lord, what's going on?" He spoke to me and said, "Pray out loud." I spoke into the room and said, "Are you guys awake?" They all said yes. I then said, "Would you mind if I prayed out loud?" It was very eager answers from them all. "No, go ahead."

Am I My Brother's Keeper?

I prayed this prayer out loud. "Lord, I can feel an evil spirit in this room, will you please remove it and replace it with your spirit?" Instantly, the spirit of the Lord was in the room, and it was almost lit up with an effervescent feeling. The peace that came into that room was beyond human comprehension. We basked in it for the next minutes and all of us peacefully went to sleep in His presence. The next morning, we got up and ate and went to work. Kind of forgetting about the incident the night before, I just went back to one of the back bedrooms and began hanging pieces of Sheetrock. A little while later, Bobby came back there and said, "Last night, I asked Jesus into my heart." Plus we discussed the evil spirit that had come into the room. We had felt it and also felt the Lord's Holy Spirit replace it. I was ecstatic inside and was so glad for the peace that Bobby now was exhibiting. He radiated with the light of the Lord all over him. The day went by so quickly. That night, the other two guys and Bobby decided to go downtown and get a room so they could shower and have a real bed. They said they would be back in the morning for work. I said okay. The next morning, the other two guys came to the house for work and told me that Bobby had decided to go to Gillette last night to tell his girlfriend about this new event. He just wanted her to know how happy he was now about allowing Jesus into his life. A little while later, a gentleman came to the door and asked for Mike Cooper. I said, "I am Mike Cooper." He said you have an emergency phone call over here at the golf course. I thought, *Oh no, something has happened to my grandfather*. We all knew he could pass at any time. When I got there and answered, it was my uncle Jack. He said that Bobby had fallen asleep at the wheel last night and ran off the road. He was dead.

Once again, I had many questions that I wanted answered. Mainly, "Why, Lord? Bobby had just accepted you and now he's gone." Remember, sometimes the answer comes simultaneously with the question. It was there during the asking. "This was allowed to do a work in the family to bring many to me." Now this is where trust and faith come into being. Can I trust this newfound God to know what is best? Yes. If we truly believe in the God of the Bible, then we know He is trustworthy and has the ultimately best plan in the universe. He alone has all the facts. We don't have even a small percentage of the facts, just a few here and there.

I went back home to share the good news with my entire family, and I knew it would help soften the blow of this untimely death. I shared the entire story and how the evil spirit came to kill and destroy. How Bobby had decided to allow the Holy Spirit to enter him instead of the evil one. We all cried tears of sorrow and joy. Losing Bobby was devastating. Knowing he was in heaven was a lot of comfort. All my other brothers and sisters, my father, stepmom, grandfather, and grandmother—all got baptized and saved. Many in the family came to faith in the Lord. He was correct in saying that it was "to do a work in the family." I was shown early in my walk with Him that He was faithful and could be trusted to do the best thing. He has our eternal interests at heart and wants the ultimate best for us. He has great plans for us. Not to harm us. To comfort us and bless us. Will we allow it?

As I look back in my life, I see the many hundreds of times that God's hand was fully involved in my daily life because I wanted Him to be, even sometimes when I didn't want Him to be. I generally ask Him to be with me. He has been more than faithful and has exceeded my greatest expectations. He knows the entire future so He can make the best long-term decisions for and about us. A prayer does not need to be long and extravagant. It can be as simple as just saying, "Lord, please come into my life." Countless thousands have said that, and the results are astounding.

Even a thief on the next cross over from Jesus was saved due to asking Jesus to please remember him. The Lord will not reject a repentant plea. He does, however, resist the proud. Where will you stand?

O, That Smell

My wife's mother was a prayer warrior and was very strong in the faith and knowledge of Jesus. She asked me one day if I would come and pray over one of her dear loved ones who was dying of cancer. I immediately was heightened by the Holy Spirit and prompted to say yes. It was a couple hours away by car, and during the entire time, I had many thoughts of what I would say over the dying woman. My faith swelled up and down, and I thought we would see a miracle that day. As we approached the room, I sensed the Holy Spirit was already there, and the room had a glow to it. As we entered, I could smell the smell of death hanging heavily in the room. It is a foul, pungent, and unmistakable sting in the nose. It makes a statement about death that nothing else can replace. Others were there and praying already, so I waited my turn and was repulsed by that smell.

Finally, it was evident that someone else could step up, and so I did. It was hard to put my hand on her, but after I did, I started praying. During that prayer, the Holy Spirit took over and transformed that smell into one of the most beautiful aromatic smells I had ever encountered. Like hundreds of roses had been brought into the room. I even looked around to see if someone had brought in flowers. They hadn't. It was the Lord's presence, and then I realized that is how He was smelling it—a fragrant and wonderful smell that wafted up to heaven to signal the coming of one of His saints. Repulsive to us, but amorous to Him. Later, when I shared what I smelled to my mother-in-law, she wept with tears of joy and found that calm assurance that only the Lord of Hosts can provide. Precious is the death of one of His saints.

Discernment

There was a time when the dividing line between good and evil was a little bit obscured. No longer true. It is as sharp now as a razor blade and more defined for sure. All things are becoming more and more sided. It could be that I am getting older and have drawn those lines in my mind. When I was younger, I wondered about certain things and their classification. I was not always so sure about them. It gets easier as we get more and more discernment on all issues. How is your discernment? We have to ask for it. It can be right on or way off. It can be developed and brought into alignment that is correct and good, or we can allow it to be way off and just make excuses and think that it's okay to justify our off base remarks and thinking. The tongue is hard to tame. It's hard to control. It can do more damage than a bullet. Sometimes the damage is permanent and might not be reversible. Watch what you say, for the words you use will judge your future. It's still all part of your choice package. We have a certain technique packed in a certain compartment, and we pull it out now and then to wield it as a weapon. We even have certain superior weapons in our arsenal that we don't know how to use. They are lethal and can cause great harm. Think before you speak and choose kind words that build up and not tear down. Words that do no harm, but bring about good. We will all give an account of every word we have ever uttered after our age of accountability. Obviously, when I was a child, I spoke as a child. When I became an adult, I put away childish things. Did you? It's not too late. If you are reading this, it's still not too late. Ask the eternal God of the universe directly for any and all help that you need, and He will answer you if you ask in a believing mode. If you don't believe it, then you are in denial. The same God has said, "I have put it into man's heart to know there is a God." Somewhere down inside of you, you know there is a God. Once you admit to yourself that you know it, then you can turn to Him and ask. No intellect or proud spirit will conquer God. His ways and thoughts are not like ours. His ways and thoughts are farther above ours than we can imagine. He is infinitely wise and thoughtful.

His love will dominate this entire universe. He wanted to share this beautiful thing called life, and He will not be defeated in that goal. He does, however, have certain rules and laws that will be followed, and they will not be compromised. There is no shortcut that will circumvent the entire plan. Line upon line, precept upon precept, it will all be orderly and done to His specifications. And we will see that His specs are the best. We will all give a big ooh or aah on that day of revelation. All things will become clear to us, and all the facts will be revealed. Our joy will be upgraded to the nth degree. Will you take a minute right now and pray for wisdom? Ask for discernment and guidance. If you haven't already, ask Jesus to cleanse you from sin and save your soul. Ask Him to be your savior and enter your heart for eternity. He will do it if you want it.

Lit Up

We say they are lit up a little if a person has been drinking alcohol. We even think it's okay to indulge in the use of that poison. We say that we should limit it and control it, but the reality is that we cannot control it. We allow our mind to be changed by it. Once changed, we defend it and even justify it. I hear some quote the Bible to get everyone over to their thinking about the wine. Just remember, we have the ability to justify all things that we want to use or have. The human mind is able to bring anything it wants to bear into its realm without remorse and computes those things to its own advantage. We are slanted and biased in more than a few things. I have the freedom to do as I please, but I choose to please the Father rather than my fleshly body.

One night, I got on my knees by my bed and began to pray to the Father. After a few minutes, I realized the room was lit up like it was almost daylight in there. It was a glowing light and had comfort in it. There were no shadows in it, and I knew it was the presence of the Lord. If I am going to be lit up, I pray it is with the light of the Holy Spirit, and not with any other spirit.

During a dream one night, while sitting against a log in a meadow, I saw a flash of light fly by me several times. It then landed on the other side of the log from me, and I immediately realized it was the Holy Spirit. I was in the presence of the third person of the trinity. He is royalty to say the least. I could hardly look at Him. I did though, and He was very beautiful. He had shoulder-length hair that was curvy and well kept. His features were both masculine and feminine at the same time. He is gracious and nonthreatening. No words were necessary, and we shared thoughts. He wore a long flowing robe that went to the ground and glowed with purity. As I gazed at Him, I longed to be with Him from now on. He then departed in a flash, and I was in awe at this encounter.

Sometimes we can't express ourselves very well, and that's okay. We might not know all the facts or understand everything, and that's okay too. We might not have the words to convey an idea or a known thought. That is okay also. But let me express to you what is not okay. It is not okay to not try. It is not okay to deny the truth that we know down deep. It is not okay to give up without an honest attempt. It is not okay to choose to be unteachable. It is not okay to turn your back on the one that gave His all for you. Turn to Him face-to-face, and don't start running away again. Pray until you hear from Him. Don't give up.

Stilts

When I was young, I watched my father and uncles walk on stilts for taping drywall. It looked fun, and I decided to make some stilts of my own, and they were awesome. They were about two feet tall and had some wooden blocks nailed on for my feet to rest on. Then I decided they weren't tall enough. I made some out of the ten-foot two-by-fours. I sat on the peak of the garage while my brother tied my legs on to the top of them. He held on to them while I stood up. I took one step and down I went onto the gravel driveway. Skinned a lot of skin off the palms of my hands and forearms, I then deducted that if I would have had a parachute, it would have slowed me down from falling so fast. So I took a large piece of heavy plastic and held on to each corner while I jumped off the garage roof to test my theory. *Bam*, down to the ground so fast and skinned up again. We do learn, but it has a price. We can try it again if we like, but it doesn't come out different if we use the same methods and the same thinking. I love the quote by Einstein, "Madness is doing the same thing over and over and expecting different results." I never jumped off the garage again, and I used real factory made stilts and got good on them eventually.

Plan A

Time has a way of proving out the truth in all things. Eventually, it is evident that only the truth prevails. Caesar said, "What is truth?" He was face-to-face with it that day when he had to judge Jesus. But he didn't have all the facts. He didn't know much about this man from Galilee, and he was allowing the Jews who were the rulers of the time to sway him and push him. His wife had warned him to avoid pronouncing judgment on Jesus, but he was caught in somewhat of a trap. He knew he must be involved in the final decision of Jesus's fate, and he tried to let him go free. Other factors were in play that only God knew about. The prophets had hinted about it in the Holy Scriptures, and Jesus had spoken privately about it a few times to His disciples. It was plan A. Nothing had changed about the plan since its inception so long ago. God knew the plan from before the creation of anything. He didn't have to ad-lib, alter, or add to the plan at any time for any reason. The plan was all set in His mind and still is. He knew the end from the beginning and has prophesied accordingly. He has given us His word at the times that we needed the word. Read the book of Daniel sometime and compare it with the book of Revelations.

An earth, a solar system, and a universe surrounding it. That is what He used. Us having an earthly body with all the temptations and the entire realm of evil exposed and exploited right in front of our eyes; is the shortest and best route to the orderly and pure life that the Holy God desired in the first place. Allowing the weeds to grow beside the wheat. Don't uproot them too early or you destroy the good crop. All the alternatives were considered—all of them. This plan was chosen in infinite wisdom. God will not be defeated in His purpose and will have the maximum yield for the sowing of His seed. He knew there was a price to pay, and He also knew that only He could pay it (Matt. 13:24–30).

Dialogue

God has spoken to man numerous times and in various ways. He is very verbal and exact about what He wants us to know. Since the Word is a living entity, it has been easy to record all that was spoken. The Word never dies and never lies to us. To know the Word is to know God Himself. We should be careful what we allow ourselves to hear. Lyrics and books contain ideas that can take us away from the intent of God's heart. Be aware of the serpent's dialogue, but don't believe it for one moment. His goal is to deceive us and cause separation from God.

All scripture is given by inspiration of God, and is profitable for doctrine, reproof, correction, for instruction in righteousness; that the men and women of God may be perfect, thoroughly furnished onto all good works (2 Tim. 3:16).

Reading the Bible is good, but the one that does what it says will find great joy. Knowing what it says and doing what it says is vastly different. Be a doer of the Word. Study and show yourself approved, a workman that does not need to be ashamed.

Vision

We can only see what comes to our eye. Our eye doesn't reach out with its own power. The light travels to us from some other place. God, however, has many types of vision and sees all things at all times. He has x-ray, infrared, and other types of vision. Nothing is hidden from Him. He can even see into your heart and discern your thoughts and motives. Nothing escapes his vision and knowledge. Be sure your sin will be known by all the host of heaven. What we would hold in secret, God will shout from the mountaintop.

Speaking of heaven, no one in heaven will be limping from a bad knee or ankle. No one will have a cold or fever. No one there will be missing a foot or hand. There will be total trust and brutal honesty. Nothing will be sore or painful. You can't get lost over there; nor can you fall down, unless it's to worship the Lord God. I choose to worship Him due to Him being worthy of my worship. Only He will be famous. God equals one. God plus His Son equals one. God plus His Holy Spirit equals one. God plus you equals one. God plus me equals one. God is one.

We all together will make one. One spirit, one mind, one life—all are *one*. Each one is a facet of the infinite God. Combined with Him, we are fulfilled. Without Him, we are nothing. Our desire is for Him, and someday we will finally see it. He is our all-fulfilling destiny. We can walk into Him and then out of Him to fulfill His purposes. If our will is to walk in Him, then we can become complete. If we fulfill our own purposes, we deny ourselves the completion that we so desire. We won't have the contentedness, peace of mind, or happiness we want unless we surrender to His will for our life.

I could tell you a thousand times a day for a thousand days and you wouldn't get it unless you ask for yourself. I can't do it for you. Only you control your eternal destiny. Choose today to give all and receive all.

www.ingramcontent.com/pod-product-compliance
Lightning Source LLC
Chambersburg PA
CBHW052117070526
44584CB00017B/2524